A
Short and Simple
Book
for the
Why's

By
Gail Hugman

Published by
The Endless Bookcase Ltd.
71 Castle Road, St Albans, Hertfordshire,
England, UK, AL1 5DQ.

www.theendlessbookcase.com

Printed Edition
Also available in multiple e-book formats via The
Endless Bookcase website, Amazon, Nook and
Kobo.

Printed in the United Kingdom
First Printing, 2016

ISBN: 978-1-908941-63-3

Dedications

This book is dedicated to all those young lives who
have enriched my own and taught me so much,
to all the lovely teachers who believe in the
uniqueness of each child
and to all those yet to be born.

The first WHY - the reason for this book:

This book started as a letter to my headteacher.

When I decided to stop teaching in schools, my headteacher asked me to tell him what I did that made the difference.

It took me six months to figure it out.

I wrote it down as a letter to send to him, but then it developed into this little book and after giving it to him, I decided to publish it for parents because I want to help. They not only have to deal with everything the world throws at them; they also have to deal with everything the world throws at their children.
It's an awesome undertaking and I take my hat off to them.

A small collection of Gail's true narrative poems can be found at the end of this book in the section titled "Nurturing the Best in Children" which follows the Postscript.
They have been included to illustrate the way that these lessons can be observed and applied in life situations.

About the author

'A Short and Simple Book for the Why's' draws on Gail's teaching and life experience. She says it took her at least 15 years to understand how children work and think and then another 15 years to work out what they need at core to help them excel. Parents do not have this time advantage. As soon as a child is born, they have to 'hit the ground running' and many are dogged by doubt and worry about the way they are raising their children. Gail's books hold the lessons, tips, reasons and activities that she has found helpful in encouraging children's core development and causing them to excel, giving them a sense of purpose, satisfaction and responsibility. Happy at core.

Gail started teaching in 1974. It was pre-National Curriculum. Teachers were very much left to their own initiative and devices in the Social Priority Area school where her teaching began in Haringey.

Gail's first classroom had 200 bibles, a stock cupboard which was so full of scrap you could barely move and little else apart from 38 mixed ability year 6 children. This was where she feels her teacher training *really* began. Gail learned very quickly to be resourceful and creative within the dynamic of teaching.

Now forty years later, the whole world of education - and society - has changed beyond recognition. The National Curriculum has set down expectations which increase almost annually; the World Wide Web is an intricate part of every classroom and teaching methods; there is far more testing than before; children have access to a much greater range of activities and resources than ever and teachers look to parents for motivating and reinforcing behaviour in their children.

This rapid period of change in human behaviour and history, poses a number of complex questions. What should we be teaching a developing child, about themselves and their future? Why do so many children disengage from school, lack confidence or have low self-esteem? Why do we have challenges with behaviour and attitude if the young have 'inquiring minds and a thirst of knowledge?'

In the first 30 years, Gail's experience included class teaching, covering the full primary range; she ran a unit for disruptive pupils in Islington for 3 years; worked with children with special needs and held various senior management roles working primarily in inner city schools.

Gail's extensive experience in schools includes teaching for one year in the USA and being an observer in schools in Israel, South Africa and Mauritius. (From this she reports that playgrounds sound the same wherever you are in the world!) This, coupled with her more recent private work with children in their homes has given her a unique perspective on the real issues faced by young learners and their parents.

In 2005, Gail created Lessons Alive as a teaching and development service. From her extensive research, experience and observation, Gail creates new and insightful workshops for parents and teachers on topics such as:

- Listening
- Concentration
- Comprehension
- Organisation
- Motivation
- Homework

helping them to motivate, inspire and empower children to take responsibility and engage in a meaningful and purposeful way in their education and development.

Birth to puberty is the foundation building phase of life and Gail believes it is therefore crucial that parents, teachers and children appreciate as fully as they can the processes involved during this period; how to set expectations and how to do the best job they can for each child.

Website: www.lessonsalive.com

Email: gail@lessonsalive.com

Preface

This is a revision of the original 'A Short and Simple Book for the Why's' written in 2001.

Since then, I have established my teaching service, Lessons Alive, which continues to maintain the very highest standard of bespoke 1-2-1 teaching for children up to the age of 11 years.

I have met, taught and re-aligned some of the most demanding children leading them to happiness and satisfaction in themselves and independence and success in their schooling.

I believe the world is in a state of change – this is not necessarily 'a bad thing'. We are built to be adaptable and creative and if we strengthen the inner core and educate children about themselves, their purpose and how things work, I believe we can help them stay true to themselves. Showing the children how to develop skills and working with them on the messages in this book will help them remain intact as they grow. As a teacher, I know from experience that these messages form the missing link between motivation and learning and can be a powerful factor in how well a child concentrates, listens, takes responsibility, behaves and performs in school and in life.

Introduction

This writing is intended to offer a way for teachers, parents and carers of primary aged children to perhaps improve the quality of life not only for themselves but more importantly for the children whose futures they are helping to build.

Experience has taught me to understand that many of the questions children want to ask they cannot verbalise and so they cry out in their behaviour. Punishment and the increasing use of behaviour management drugs such as Ritalin are clearly not the answer and we are facing an unprecedented crisis in our schools which can only get frighteningly worse.

Parents and colleagues throughout the years have admired my results with children not simply because of their academic achievement but also because of the way the children developed in confidence and stature. Often I have been asked about my classroom organisation, but I do not think that is where the answer lies.

I believe that part of my success lay in the fact that I did not expect children to necessarily realise things that are obvious to me as an adult. They are **learning** to think, **learning** to draw conclusions, **learning** to weigh evidence and when each child walked through my classroom door, what I was looking at was not just 'another kid', but a young representative of the highest form of intelligent organic life on this planet, trying to assemble itself as best it could and with a most brilliant opportunity and journey ahead of it. I wanted to help that in any way that I could and felt extremely privileged to be in that position.

I have now come to believe that there are fundamental truths and a few simple facts that each child needs to be given in order to properly equip them for their journey through life. This book attempts to put forward a few of these simple truths and if these are given to children, I believe the increasing distress and self-destructive behaviour we see erupting in our schools and society in general, may be quelled. I hope that it is not too late, though for some, I fear it may be.

Therefore, if you agree with what you read, next time you are with children and the opportunity presents itself, please, using a little care and sensitivity; pass on some of these messages. They are simple and effective, can only be of benefit in boosting self-esteem, standards and values and the children will love and thank you for making some sense out of the chaos in which they find themselves.

You are <u>the</u> most
intelligent,
talented
and
versatile form of life on
this planet.

You can be very proud of this and let it show
in
your behaviour
by,
for example,
keeping
yourself clean and tidy
and
by helping
others whenever you are
able to do so.

On the next page is a summary of the evidence to
support natural human versatility – making this
conscious in children helps them feel accomplished and
confidence begins to grow.

An Alphabet of Evidence
or
'Some of what a human CAN DO'

Act   Admire   Animate   Agree   Allow
Believe   Bring   Blow   Beckon
Care   Clean   Collect   Create   Carry
Dance   Deny   Deliver
Energise   Enchant   Empathise
Forgive   Formulate   Fly aeroplanes
Gather   Grow   Grin   Generate
Help   Hide   Honour
Initiate   Imitate
Join   Jump   Joke
Keep   Knit   Kiss
Love   Labour   Live   Lead   Like   Laugh
Mother   Mark   Maintain   Measure
Nurture   Notice
Observe   Obey   Offer   Order
Pacify   Perceive   Praise   Petition   Poise   Prove
Question   Quiet   Quicken   Quote
Rush   React   Recall   Recognise
Search   Speak   Sell
Talk   Twirl   Tumble   Trim   Try   Trust
Understand   Untie   Unite
Value   View   Voice
Weep   Wait   Watch   Wish   Welcome
X-ray!
Yawn   Yell   Yearn
Zap!

Apart from you, your body
contains all the tools you
need to experience life.

You have been given a brain,
an instinct,
emotion,
five senses,
a soul
and
a spirit.

They all have different jobs to do and are
the most important gifts you have.
If you are careful, they will serve you well.
You are meant to use them to build yourself
inside
-
that is why each person is different although
we are all given the same equipment.

Look out of a window
and try to think
how many blades of grass
there are on this planet,
how many leaves on each tree,
how many fish,
how many people.
Each and every single one is a
BEST EFFORT
by whatever
created it.
Let each action you make
be the same.

You are one of the luckiest little people on this earth.

You know that you will be fed today,
you know that you have a bed to go to,
you know that you can get a drink of water
when you need it.
Remember to thank those who provide for
you and
be grateful for what you have.

There are children, just like you, who
- as you hear this, right now -
are not in your position.

There are children who do not have homes,
do not have parents,
do not have school to give them an
education, do not have a meal each day.

(This needs to be thought through and delivered
carefully, being sensitive to the circumstances of the
children being addressed. Never-the-less, **all** the children
can be told what there is to be grateful for.)

You only get one life

-

it's yours.

It's not your parents, they have their own.
It's not your teachers, they have their own.
It's not your friends, they have their own
too.

It's your life.
It is unique
and it has a purpose.

Make the most of it by being the best you
can be at any time.

If you are ten years old, be the best ten year
old you can be (otherwise you might not be
ready for eleven when it comes!)

Try to do well in
school because it
is the place where
people will try to give
you
the skills and knowledge
you need to be able to look after yourself
later on.

School
is not the reason
for your life, but you have to go to
school because that
is the law which tries to give everyone a fair
opportunity.

It's important to remember that there isn't
time at school to tell you everything you
need to
know about living.

Everyone and every thing
on the planet is governed
by natural laws.

If you fall out of bed, you drop on the floor!
That is a natural law at work.

Try to discover the laws by looking at nature
and
the way things work – science is brilliant for
this.

(Adults don't always realise that the task of
learning to read can be quite overwhelming for some
children who think that there are millions of letters to
learn. Demonstrating the repetitious use of one letter on
a page of writing can be a real revelation for such
children.)

Did you know there are only twenty six
letters
in the English alphabet?
Once you know them you will be able to
read any book in English
any time, anywhere in the world.

The alphabet is another toolbox
and each letter represents
a sound you can make.

You are so clever; you already knew all the
sounds
when you were a few months old.

(Maths can pose similar difficulties for some children.)

There are
only
nine numbers
in the whole,
wide
world.

They are:

1
2
3
4
5
6
7
8
9

and all that we can do is make them
BIGGER
and
smaller.

Remember that while
you are young
it is easy to
change
because you
haven't finished
building
yourself.

So, if you make a mistake,
say sorry if you need to
(even to yourself)
and change
–
by doing it
a
different way.

There's
enough
fighting and unpleasantness
in the
world
without
you
adding
to
it.

It gives whatever made us the wrong
impression
about what we want.

Never stop asking questions.
You may meet a person
who can answer them
one day
(and that person might just turn out to be
yourself!)

It is harder for an adult
to change so be careful
about the habits
you grow.

Grow good habits which will
help
you in your life.

(Being proud to be human is a good habit to
grow!
Being thorough in all you do is another good
habit
to grow – you never see a half finished
snowflake
do you?)

The most important
gift you will
have in your life is
that you will be able to
CHOOSE.

While you are learning how to make your
own choices,
if you are lucky, your parents (and some
other adults like teachers) will make them
for you.

You might not like the choices they make for
you but choosing is a very
responsible thing to do and it is not always
easy.

There are many things
in this world and in
your life that
you cannot
see
but
that you can
feel
because they are
real.

Like magnetism, electricity, your thoughts
and ideas, your energy, warmth, excitement,
sadness, anticipation, missing mum and dad,
hunger, a sense of satisfaction, and
tiredness.

Trust your instinct
and more may
be revealed to you.

**Postscript
for those who
are entering the
Teaching Profession**

It has always given me great pleasure to work with student teachers and those entering the profession of which I am so proud to be a part. It is now time for me to move on in my own life and development and I have made the decision to leave the classroom.

For those who follow, I have this to say.

Teaching is not about league tables and test results as a first principle. Teaching is about playing a part in the formation and development of fresh young lives, baffled by the complexities of modern living.

It means developing the arts and skills which will enable you to transmit enthusiasm and radiate an infectious desire for learning so that those you teach know they are secure. When you are able to do this, you will see their confidence flourish because they will know that you are human, that their mistakes will cost them nothing apart from the value of the learning involved and that they are valued for what they are and not judged for what they are not. They know how much there is to learn and they fear the consequences of their own inadequacies.

As teachers we wield an awesome influence upon the lives who look to us for leadership and instruction. We have a duty of care to exercise that influence responsibly.

As you set your feet upon the path that I have trodden. I wish you well. You have so much to look forward to – I have enjoyed the good lessons and tried to correct the not so good ones when I spotted them. I have not tried to be perfect, I have only tried to improve, year on year, and I have been successful to a certain extent, but there is always more to learn and always more to improve.

I was once told that real intelligence is knowing your situation at any time. It is not difficult to see that our situation is a very precarious one and we are threatening our own existence. Look at any young life and it is clear, we are not born with competition, with gain and loss, with jealousy and greed.

I do not believe that one day a magic wand will wave and put it right. I see we all have the same basic equipment with which to experience and develop. I therefore believe that we do not need to perpetuate the mistakes of the past, but that we can each have a hand in turning the tide of our own future by what we choose to promote in ourselves and those around us.

It is my belief that you can have a great part to play in nurturing what is real and of value in those you teach. Promote only the best of what is natural in a human – respect, enthusiasm, fascination, dignity, pride, high standards, a wish to do well, and above all, a value for the privilege of having been given life. Learn from yourself. Let your instinct guide you, learn from the responses children give you, believe in what you are doing and it may be that one day, you will turn around and see that their world is a better place because you are in it. Good luck.

My notes

A page for you.

My notes

A page for you.

Nurturing the Best in Children

Each story illustrates an example of a compelling observation in action; for clarification, these observations and understandings are extracted and precede the story that encapsulates them.

Each story is also true and there may be some readers who recognise themselves within them – if that is the case – "HELLO! You have not been forgotten, and nor will you ever be."

True stories from this life of mine
For when you have a little time....

To Begin

There is no introduction but
What you may need to know
Lies written on pages here within
To help each youngster glow.

The natural world around us
Is ordered, clearly planned
Within it all, it's plain to see
That Greatness had a hand

The natural laws that govern
The patterns of life on earth
Are like an unseen guide book
From the moment of our birth

And yet within each human
The natural seems to fade
As travelling through our childhood
A different mould is made

And if you tend the seeds of this
Just listen to your heart,
For truth will always find a way
And it must play its part.

The future is unfolding
And may be much improved,
If reading 'twixt the lines of this
You let yourself be moved.

Read on now, very carefully,
Be thorough in what you do
And watch for some surprises
That may happen inside of you.

**It is important
to be
clear
in what you say
to children
else you
confuse
the
natural system and introduce
warp**

A child of two with great delight
Leapt from his mother's knee,
And ran to touch a little dog,
Who from the child did flee

Alarmed the mother cried to me,
As to the door he ran
"Stop him, please, look out!" she said
Then to the child began

"You naughty boy, that's very bad,"
I knew just what she meant,
But from my observation
That wasn't why he went

And so without her meaning it -
From fear and good intention -
The mother confused the little boy
By practicing invention

**Trust
is an
in-built
natural
quality
-
we all
have it
when we
close our eyes
each
night**

I took some girls away from home
I warned them of the dangers
"You must be very careful please,
And do not talk to strangers"

We stopped on our long journey
For a loo break and a rest,
As the children went away from us
I saw it as a test

I am sure you can imagine
The fear that shot through me
As talking to a stranger
Several children I did see

I rushed then to remind them
Their memories for to jog

"We were not talking to him, Miss
We were talking to his dog!"

We must be very mindful then
As I came to realise,
The dangers look so different
When viewed through children's eyes

Our values are instrumental
in determining
behaviour.
We learn them when we're young.

We are not born with values
We have to build them in
And children need some guidance
This is how I did begin.

Each year the children came to me
I'd look around and say
Who sees there's someone in the class
With whom you never play?

It always would surprise me
After many a primary year
That each child in the class could point
To others they never went near.

It was not through squabbles or dislike
That they had never mixed
Just habit and lack of reason
To the same friends they were fixed.

And so for several lessons
We would make it quite a game,
To sit beside a 'stranger'
And learn more than just their name.

How many brothers, sisters too,
What they did and didn't
Like to do
What made them laugh,
What made them cry,

Their favourite foods,
And all their moods
We sat an hour and each would ask
We made it quite a little task.

And at the end of all of this
We found we'd learnt a lot
So we gathered it together
To look at what we'd got.
We always had some good at maths,
On whom we could rely
We had them good at English too
"I'll help you", they'd reply

Others played up different gifts
The rare one
- giving spiders lifts
(We always had a fearless spider monitor for
removal purposes)

We valued too
A clever clown
Who'd make us laugh
When we were down

And gradually it dawned on us
That each of us was needed,
Without someone we weren't complete
So cries for help were heeded.

It only takes a little thought
A little time and care
To place good values in young lives
And watch them blossom there.

When working with children,
it is important
to be
open, sensitive, reflective and firm,
to know who and what *you* are,
and to
carry in yourself
the qualities and standards
you seek to nurture
in them –
else you will add
to the confusion
with which they are struggling.

Alone, we cannot change the world
The problems are too great,
But we can change ourselves inside
Perhaps it's not too late

To rise above all judgement
All criticism and more
It's not an easy thing to do
When reaching for the core.

Life is a glittering promise
We're only given once,
And if we do not use it
There is no other chance.

So look to your own talents
They're yours alone to grow

And when you find the truth of you
The evidence will show.

This is what children should receive
They're born into the real
But with deception all around
Confusion's what they feel.

Without this education
What future here on earth?
The potential of magnificence
Awaits us from our birth.

BV - #0016 - 081223 - C0 - 210/148/3 - PB - 9781908941633 - Gloss Lamination